The Gentleman's Farm

SHIRLEY PLANTATION

Charles City County
Mr. and Mrs. Charles Hill Carter III
Operated in association with The Shirley Plantation Foundation

"Shirley is a family home that we share with the public, not some stagnant version of history," reflects Charles Hill Carter III, seated with his wife, Lauren, on a stone terrace overlooking land that has been part of the Carter legacy for eleven generations. A portrait from c. 1700, now hanging in the great house at Shirley, depicts Edward Hill IV (1690–1706) as a boy in classical garb, gesturing toward an idealized version of the same pastoral landscape. Charles nods "Agriculture is in our blood."[1]

In 1613 Sir Thomas West, third Lord Delaware and royal governor of Virginia, received a land grant from James I of England and named a four-thousand-acre tract of his Virginia property in honor of his wife, Lady Cessalye Sherley. After West's death, Edward Hill I, a member of Virginia's House of Burgesses and the ancestor of the current residents, was granted 450 fertile riverside acres of the plantation in 1638; with the proceeds earned over a lifetime in the lucrative tobacco trade, he bought more than 2,500 additional acres. In 1723 his grandson, Edward Hill III, began construction on a new, grand house facing the James River, the primary artery for communication, enabling up to nine-tenths of the plantation's crops to reach market.[2] Edward's daughter, Elizabeth, and her husband, John Carter—eldest son of Robert "King" Carter, the wealthiest man in America—inherited the property in 1726 and completed the house we know today as Shirley.

When the Carters moved into their new house in 1738, the residence was not merely grand in its own right, but stood as the centerpiece of a complex of buildings designed to serve the functions of the plantation, and was visually refined by Dutch and Anglo-Palladian notions of formality of design. The distinctive verticality of Shirley was moderated, in its original form, by the weight of symmetrical, flanking, three-story outbuildings, located thirty-six feet from either side of the main block. These outbuildings isolated the laborious work of plantation life from the ceremonial and private activities of the family in the main house. In addition to housing a laundry and kitchen, each with sleeping quarters above, these outbuildings defined a working courtyard in the shadow of the great house. A 1742 plat map of Shirley shows even more structures, including a bake house, blacksmith's house, boathouse, tobacco sheds, and "great quarters," a dormitory for enslaved field workers. Two privies were artfully concealed by plantings in the gardens. Remarkably, seven dependencies built during the original construction period of 1723 to 1738 survive today, including the icehouse, laundry, and stable, as well as a pump house added in the 1770s.[3]

Generations of Carter descendants placed their stamp on the house, refining its details to conform to the taste of their own day. In 1771, following Elizabeth Hill Carter's death, her son Charles embarked on extensive updates, replacing the tile roof with slate, and adding the fashionable, Palladian-inspired

PRECEDING PAGES *The great house at Shirley, built 1723–26, has been in the Carter family for eleven generations. The current generation continues to work the land.*

RIGHT *The remarkable "flying staircase" rises three stories without visible support above the entrance hall, embellished with ancestral portraits.*

porticos, shutters, and casement windows to the exterior, as well as embellishing the interior with distinguished paneling and ornamental woodwork.

As was true for many of Virginia's early plantations, tobacco culture drained the soil at Shirley of nutrients by the mid-eighteenth century, but, unlike smaller farms where every square inch of soil was needed just for subsistence, Shirley was home to experiments in crop rotation that heralded a new generation of agriculture. The Carters introduced legumes to restore nitrogen to the soil, so that some tobacco could continue to be produced. But in 1817 Hill Carter burned Shirley's tobacco barns and focused his efforts instead on raising wheat and cotton. The tobacco era of two centuries ended without sentiment, because, as today's Charles Carter notes, "In agriculture, survival depends on managing what you have." Three years later, in 1820, lightning struck and destroyed the original north flanker building. In the spirit of adaptability, Hill Carter salvaged the vaulted basement and converted it into a root cellar (which remained in use until World War II). In the 1830s, as cotton came to define Southern agriculture, the original columns of Shirley's great house were replaced with new ones in the Doric order, a stylish nod to then-current Greek Revival taste.

In 1847 Edmund Ruffin, "the father of American agronomy," purchased neighboring Evelynton. Ruffin, perhaps best remembered today as a radical pro-secessionist and the man who fired the first shot on Fort Sumter, was also a pioneer in scientific farming, including the refinement of practical soil testing to help farmers target fertilizer application to address specific nutrient deficiencies. His publications, most notably as editor of *The Farmer's Register* (published monthly from 1833 until 1842), advocated for reformed agricultural practices in the South, and while he may not have succeeded in changing centuries-old habits across the region, his work did encourage new

ownership of John Eyre, Severn's grandson, that Eyre Hall developed into the eighteenth-century estate we now know.

John Eyre lived at his family estate for sixty-six years. He is credited with expanding the two-story wing on the east end of the original house (completed in two phases: 1795, 1805), as well as developing the ornamental gardens (1800) and constructing the orangerie (1818). Although not a merchant, John held mercantile interests as well as extensive landholdings. Having abandoned tobacco, Eyre grew corn, oats, peas, and other cash crops and raised livestock. All of this created an "ample fortune," as duly noted on his tombstone, and made Eyre the epitome of the gentleman farmer. At his death he was recalled as "a model for the man of fortune and the Virginia gentleman."[11] In 1800 he married Ann Upshur of Accomack County, and together they ushered in a period of Federal elegance at Eyre Hall.

The house's wide side passage, entered from the southern portico, runs the entire depth of the house and is divided by an elliptical archway into a front entry hall and a rear stair hall. In the eighteenth century most guests would have gotten no farther in the house, but they would have been impressed with the finishes and furnishings that attested to the obvious good taste of the owner. This space, featuring twelve-foot ceilings, was used for entertaining, as evidenced by the presence of many musical instruments, and as a summer living space, cooled by doors opening to all

A wide, elliptical archway divides the side passage entrance hall from the stairhall. This highly social space was used for entertaining and was furnished to impress guests.

Still, the tone of Washington's long missive to Anderson was undoubtedly that of a leader: strategic, practical, and leaving little to anyone's discretion. It provided field-by-field instructions on rotating clover, timothy, rye, wheat, corn, peas, and buckwheat, as well as turnips, potatoes, pumpkins; instructions on composting and preparing manure for field use; when and how to pen and feed oxen, mules, cattle, sheep, and pigs, and where and how to construct or repair fencing. While he voiced concerns about cleanliness and good order, it was as a practical farmer and not a landscape gardener that Washington addressed his managers:

These are the great out lines of a Plan, and the operations of it, for the next year, and for years to come. . . . The necessary arrangements, and all the preparatory measures for carrying it into effect, ought to be adopted without delay, and invariably pursued.

PRECEDING PAGES *The iconic entrance facade of Mount Vernon stood at the center of a bustling complex of working farm buildings (pp. 36–37).*

ABOVE *The "new" kitchen (1775) is connected to the*

main house by covered arcades. Enslaved workers prepared food here and lived upstairs.

ABOVE *Washington dressed, read, conducted affairs of state, and managed his farm from his study (added 1774).*

Smaller matters may, and undoubtedly will, occur occasionally; but none, it is presumed, that can militate against it materially.[26]

Washington, punctual by military habit and by nature, arrived back at Mount Vernon just before the midday supper at three o'clock, his hair caked with snow and his coat soaked through from his ride across his farmland. He declined advice to change into dry clothes.[27] A gentleman never kept his guests waiting.

Starting with two thousand acres inherited from his half-brother Lawrence's estate in 1761, Washington had purchased adjacent parcels until his "five farms" in Fairfax County, including the Mount Vernon estate, comprised a massive holding of 7,400 acres, with nearly half of those actively under cultivation. Over his lifetime he actively acquired land whenever possible, certain that property was the true currency of the nation. He owned even more property—around fifty thousand acres—in the frontiers

in a venerable continuum that led, inexorably, to the new American republic and the wilderness it stood poised to conquer.

As early as 1767 Jefferson had begun to refer to the hilltop site of his (as yet unbuilt) villa, locally known as "Little Mountain," by the Italian name Monticello.[40] This apparent affectation may have been a statement of intent. In his characteristically hyperanalytical way, Jefferson believed that modern regional dialects of the Italian language were direct descendants of ancient Latin and that the Tuscan was the most authentic.[41] The primacy of Tuscan culture as a link to the ancient Romans would have been supported by the fact that the best surviving documentary evidence for the patrician *villa rustica* lay in descriptions of villas in Tuscany. And while Jefferson analyzed texts for evidence upon which to base a re-creation of the lost world of the patrician *villa rustica*, eighteenth-century artists like Giovanni Battista Piranesi (1720–78) and Allan Ramsay (1713–84), architects like Robert Adam (1728–92), and treasure hunters and gentlemen-explorers all scoured the Italian countryside for the material, archaeological remains of these fabled ancient villas.

Beyond the more codified pastoral verses romanticizing rural life such as the *Georgics* of Virgil (29 BC), Jefferson and his contemporaries would have known Cicero's (107–44 BC) accounts of his villa retreat at Tusculum and, above all, Pliny the Younger's (AD 61–c. 112) two long letters extolling the architectural and landscape features of his magnificent villas at Tusci and Laurentinum. Jefferson eventually owned three editions of these detailed, alluring, and influential accounts.[42]

PRECEDING PAGES *The temple front portico (p. 62) reflects the monumental architecture of Monroe's presidency, as well as his unconventional choice to use five columns in order to retain unobstructed views of the gardens and working fields from the double drawing room (pp. 64–65).*

THIS PAGE *According to long-standing tradition, the drawing room's marble mantel (one of a matched pair) was given to the Monroes by Lafayette following his 1825 visit.*

convenience, or simply from the overarching desire that Oak Hill appear appropriately presidential, Monroe created the house at Oak Hill in the context of the rebuilding of Washington following the British burning of the capital in 1814. He had James Hoban, architect of the White House, coordinate the project, and Washington craftsmen create the millwork in the city and ship it to Oak Hill for installation under the supervision of the farm manager. He even went so far as to follow federal pricing guidelines for materials and wage rates.[52] By the end of Monroe's second term in 1825, the accumulated debt from his properties and from entertaining (government officials were expected to pay for state occasions out of their own pockets) meant that he had to choose between his farms at Highland and Oak Hill. With a better offer on the table for Highland, Monroe chose Oak Hill as his retirement estate.[53]

At first approach, from the north, Oak Hill presents a traditional, three-part, Palladian-derived form, with a three-bay center block flanked by symmetrical wings (originally one bay wide and one story in height). The stark entrance facade—the entrance articulated with an arch rather than a portico—recalls not only Hoban's State, Navy, War, and Treasury Department buildings (none of which survives today), but also the French-tinged, radical Neoclassicism of Latrobe's Decatur House (1817) on Lafayette Square, the most fashionable residence in Washington at the time. The fact that Monroe chose to place the monumental, temple-front portico on the opposite, south side, overlooking the fields, is perhaps also a nod to the French tradition of reserving the grandest facade of a chateau for the garden front. This choice invites the viewer to stroll into the garden and turn back to enjoy the "best" view of the house, and thus defines the house's pri-

The library (above)

Furnished according to a 1776 inventory, The Blue Room (opposite), at the southeast corner of the west wing, features a dressing table as well as a bed, chest of drawers and set of seventeen prints after Rubens.

waiting only for the clasp upon her kissing wings." The story is a thinly veiled metaphor for the Reconstruction South, its heroine torn between passionate devotion to the ghost of her dead husband and desire for his look-alike (and very much alive) double. Amélie's descriptions of the plantation setting are loaded with references to mythology and folklore, animating the landscape of her childhood with the romantic grandeur of an antediluvian paradise: "October in Eden could not have been more perfect than October in Virginia."[94]

The book, which sold a stunning 300,000 copies, capitalized upon a tidal wave of nostalgia (especially among Yankees) for the idealized gentility and pastoral landscape of the vanquished antebellum South. Amélie skillfully promoted her Virginia novels, including *The Ghost Garden* and *Virginia of Virginia*, in numerous interviews and magazine profiles. These were often conducted at Castle Hill, showcasing her family's eccentricities at the venerable dynastic seat as exactly the kind of Southern Gothic mise-en-scène the public

Southwest of the main house, a fountain featuring Mercury, the Roman god of travel and exchange, greets visitors to the extensive gardens.

craved. Oscar Wilde was a fan; so were Henry James and Thomas Hardy.

Meanwhile, her Newport adventures yielded a groom, and in August 1888 in the parlor of Castle Hill she married John Armstrong "Archie" Chanler, scion of the super-wealthy, super-Yankee Astor family (with a reputed individual net worth of four million dollars). At a time when the public—or at least the press—craved a romantic metaphor for the reunion of the conquering North and the vanquished South, Archie and Amélie were the just the ticket.[95] And Archie, helpfully, contributed to the cost of some much-deferred repairs to Castle Hill. Perhaps hoping to gain some distance from his in-laws, in 1890 he purchased nearby Merrie Mill Farm, an 1857 gentleman's seat on land associated with the Walker family's pre-Revolutionary-era gristmill.[96] But Amélie and Castle Hill were inseparable. The couple traveled, fueled by his Francophilia and against her better judgment. When the marriage collapsed, in 1896, Archie went insane, but the dauntless Amélie married a half-Russian aristocrat, Prince Pierre Troubetzkoy (his mother hailed from Baltimore), whom she had met through Oscar Wilde. Archie, still smitten, continued to provide for his former wife, now a Princess, as well as, chivalrously, her prince, while friends like A.I. DuPont discreetly provided funds to support Castle Hill in its increasingly ruinous glory. For his part, Troubetzkoy gamely embraced country life, contributing income from his work as a portraitist and, when all else failed, foraging for edible greens on the lawn, appearing later in white tie for dinner to eat them.[97] Archie, having endured his own series of adventures and misfortunes, returned to live at nearby Merrie Mill, a great benefactor to the community but eventually going mad and dying there in 1935.

Troubetzkoy died the following year, but Amélie lived on at Castle Hill, a Havisham-like prisoner of her own creation (and a laudanum habit), visited by literary friends and admirers such as Ellen Glasgow, William Faulkner, and Louis Auchincloss until her death in 1945. In 1947 Castle Hill was sold out of the Rives family and has since been home to a series of devoted owners. Nevertheless, by 2005 the property was threatened with development, when it was rescued by Ray and Stewart Humiston. Not only has this couple meticulously restored the house and gardens, but they have placed the entire property under a permanent protective easement and have also donated four hundred acres of wooded mountainside to the Nature Conservancy. In 2012 Stewart Humiston and her friend Emmy-winning writer-director Hugh Wilson (a former resident of nearby Edgewood once part of the Castle Hill plantation), hit upon the idea of sharing the literary inspiration Castle Hill had offered generations of the Rives family. A series of workshops and programs has allowed aspiring writers and devoted readers to meet "local" authors, including John Grisham, Donna Lucey, actress and memoirist Sissy Spacek, and, in keeping with the Rives family tradition, historian Barclay Rives.

EDGEWOOD

Albemarle County
Al and Cindy Schornberg, Keswick Vineyards

Edgewood is a place of new beginnings, built on old traditions. Owners Al and Cindy Schornberg had been pondering a change from their busy lives in Michigan, where Al had built a successful software company, when a near fatal plane crash in 1995 spurred them into action. Al was a passionate wine connoisseur who had grown up hearing stories about his grandfather, a vintner at Massena Cellars in France; he felt that pursuing a new career in wine making would be not just a nod to his heritage, but also a way to engage the whole family. He and his wife spent several years contemplating potential vineyard properties in California and Texas be-

fore they visited Edgewood, in Albemarle County, for the first time in 2000. The rolling hills dotted with sheep and cattle, the distant views of the mountains, the whitewashed board fences—Edgewood seemed like a pastoral fantasy. And when Cindy spotted the grapevine motif in the dining room moldings, the message seemed clear: this was the place. Encouraged by the developing wine culture in Virginia, as well as the varieties of soil available for cultivation, the Schornbergs recognized Edgewood as the perfect place to experiment with new as well as tried-and-true vines and to begin a fresh chapter in their lives.

While the land at Edgewood, originally part of the Castle Hill estate, has been cultivated since at least 1737, the great house dated from 1911. It was built for New York–born ambassador George Barclay Rives and his wife, the former Gisela Preinersdorfer, whom he had met and married in Vienna in 1908.[98] A direct descendant of Nicholas Meriwether, the recipient of the 18,000-acre royal land grant in 1727 that established Castle Hill, George Barclay Rives had three children with his wife, Gisela. Two sons, Anthony Barclay (b. 1909) and George Barclay (b. 1910), had arrived by the time he stepped down from his diplomatic career, and a third son, Alexander, followed in 1916. In anticipation of his return to Virginia, Rives purchased 556 acres of land in 1906 from his widowed great-aunt Sarah, who was struggling to make a go of it at the ancestral home of Castle Hill, just across the Gordonsville Road. Not long afterward, he met architect Waddy Wood at a dinner party in Washington hosted by noted authoress, family friend—and fellow Albemarle native—Julia Magruder. When Rives was ready to settle in Virginia a few years later, he wrote to Wood from New York:

> I have part of the Castle Hill Estate, which has been in my family for so many generations, but as my part has no house I am contemplating building. I have drawn a rough sketch of the exterior, as well as the division of the interior, so that you may have a foundation on which to base your plans.[99]

PRECEDING PAGES *Davis' portrait, completed by F. Percy Wild, hangs in the Renaissance Great Hall (pp. 128–129) and shows Davis as Master of the Loudoun Hunt. Portraits of Davis' mother, Annie Morris, and his father, Thomas Gordon Davis, hang to the sides.*

OPPOSITE *The house is furnished with items the Davises procured on their travels, including Flemish Brabent tapestries, Hudson River Valley landscape painting, and braziers from Morocco and Spain.*

ABOVE *The Steinway piano Marguerite Davis received on her eighteenth birthday stands in the ladies' French drawing room.*

When the Davises purchased Morven Park, the estate already held a significant mansion, substantial stables, a fine carriage house, and a well-designed landscape. The Davises made only minor changes to the house, focusing instead on the surrounding land.

In the tradition of gentlemen farmers, Davis became intensely interested in helping to sustain and modernize Virginia's agricultural industry. He established his farm as a "testing station," where Virginia's small farmers could see proof of experimental methods and materials, without taking the financial risk themselves. He also followed in the footsteps of early Virginia farmers such as George Washington, improving the fields with fertilizer and planting cover crops, orchards, and vegetable gardens. The experimental farm consisted of purebred livestock herds, including Guernsey cattle, Percheron horses, Dorset sheep, and Yorkshire pigs—which Davis personally selected while on trips to England and Europe. Under Davis, Morven Park became one of the country's largest producers of Bronze turkeys, which had only recently become a viable domestic poultry product. He also bred numerous prizewinning racehorses. Because he had the leisure and the wealth to experiment, and could afford sometimes to fail, Davis could determine the most efficient, effective, and profitable systems of farming and then pass along that knowledge to the average farmer.[106]

Davis employed several outlets to share his knowledge. In 1907 he co-founded the Virginia Dairyman's Association, which lobbied for stricter regulation of dairy products and promoted sanitary conditions in dairy barn design. To demonstrate these principles, he improved Morven Park's own dairy barns by installing windows for light and ventilation and pouring concrete floors for sanitation. In 1909 he was named president of the Virginia Farmer's Institute, the forerunner of Virginia's Agricultural Extension Service. A few years later, Davis purchased *The Southern Planter*, an agricultural journal established in 1840, and began publishing articles on new farming practices and the results of his agricultural experiments at Morven Park. Davis' role in progressive and innovative farming techniques propelled him into statewide politics, and in 1918 he became governor of Virginia.

After his term as governor, the Davises returned to their Morven Park estate and began transforming the ornamental landscape of the property. They established a boxwood garden of their own design, consisting of five terraces planted with old-growth English and American specimens purchased and transferred from properties throughout the state.[107] When Westmoreland Davis died after suffering a stroke in 1942, he was buried in "a favorite spot in the gardens." At her death in 1963, Marguerite was buried beside her husband.[108]

Prior to her death, Marguerite Davis established the Westmoreland Davis Memorial Foundation to celebrate her husband's legacy and that of their estate. In the 1960s the house and grounds were rehabilitated, and today Morven Park serves as one of Loudoun County's prominent house museums and open spaces. It also houses the Museum of Hounds & Hunting North America and the Winmill Carriage Collection, and served for more than a decade as the headquarters for the Masters of Foxhounds Association, of which Davis was one of the founders.

Morven Park continues Davis' progressive agricultural legacy through two innovative farming programs. Through its "incubator" program, known as the Southern Planter Farm, the foundation offers acreage to aspiring farmers who want to hone their techniques and test the market for their products before making the risky, and expensive, commitment of purchasing their own property.[109] The Turkey Hill Farm is an agricultural demonstration center that promotes environmentally sensitive agriculture. For over fifty years, the foundation has provided sound and forward-thinking stewardship for the Morven Park estate.

A gentleman with a distinguished Southern lineage, Westmoreland Davis was a serious, hands-on farmer. As the editor of *Country Life in America* noted in a 1908 feature on Loudoun County, "All the raising of animals is here not the fad of men of wealth who would play at country life. It is a serious business, productive of actual profit and a deep-seated satisfaction as continuous and well-grounded as I have ever seen taken by men in their vocation."[110]

Although occupied with farming and politics, Davis was also an avid reader and his library contains biographies on famous Virginians George Washington and Robert E. Lee, novels by Winston Churchill, and his copy of Gone with the Wind.

EDGEMONT

Albemarle County
Patrick and Arlette Monteiro de Barros

Located on the eastern side of Fan Mountain, down a narrow country lane near the crossroads of Alberene, Edgemont features a jewel box–like main house derived from a late-eighteenth-century design attributed to Thomas Jefferson. The property languished in relative obscurity until the mid-1930s, when photographer Frances Benjamin Johnston and architect Milton Grigg "rediscovered" it while conducting an architectural survey for the Carnegie Institute.[124] Thus began a two-decade restoration of the property, which is now considered one of Jefferson's most notable residential works.

In the late eighteenth century, James Powell Cocke purchased 1,600 acres of the former Mildred Meriwether patent in southern Albemarle County. Cocke suffered from malaria and may have moved to Albemarle from his low-lying home at Malvern Hill, east of Richmond, to take advantage of the beneficial mountain air. Although no documentation exists, it is generally believed that Cocke enlisted Jefferson to design a home for him. Jefferson was a neighbor, with Monticello located about fifteen miles away, and Cocke was a distant cousin of James Hartwell Cocke, one of Jefferson's closest friends, supporters, and (presumed) architectural clients. By 1797, Cocke's new home was built.[125]

Placed at a prominence, the nearly square cottage overlooks the bottomlands of the Hardware River to the east. Like other Jefferson dwellings, the house is set into the hillside, so that on its entrance or west facade it appears to be a single-story house. Only when the visitor has moved to the east side of the house is it revealed that there are in fact two stories, with a garden level accessible from the lower level. The deceptive one-story appearance, the integration of the house into the landscape, the sophisticated architectural details, and the general similarities to the designs for Monticello and Poplar Forest convinced Grigg that "this is Jefferson."

When Johnston and Grigg found the house, it was in a dilapidated condition. An inappropriate kitchen addition had been built on the south end of the house and the once majestic, five-terraced garden was completely overgrown. The most recent inhabitants had been a pair of spinster sisters. When one died, the other in her mourning painted the entire house, inside and out, black.[126]

In his enthusiasm for this "forgotten" Jefferson masterpiece, Grigg wrote to Fiske Kimball, the eminent Jefferson scholar who was then serving as the head of the Philadelphia Museum of Art. Kimball, however, had already been alerted to the house's existence by an article in the Virginia Historical Society's journal and had visited the property.[127] Kimball wrote, "I came very near [buying] it—what stopped me was the fact that it would be a thirty-five mile round trip to change into evening clothes between tea and dinner at the University [of Vir-

MARRIOTT RANCH AT FAIRFIELD FARM

Fauquier County
Marriott International

The name "Marriott" has been synonymous with hospitality since 1927, when J. Willard Marriott—newly arrived in Washington, DC, from his native Utah—opened an A&W Root Beer stand on 14th Street. Soon Marriott and his new bride, Alice ("Allie") Sheets, diversified the stand into their first "Hot Shoppe," which specialized in Mexican and Southwestern-style food. Allie, fluent in Spanish, sought culinary advice and recipes from the chef at the Mexican embassy. From these beginnings, the family developed a brand that today is known worldwide.

John Willard Marriott was born on his father's sheep ranch in Marriott Settlement, Utah, in 1900. There he tended sheep and assisted with the harvest and transport of sugar beets. Marriott developed into an avid horseman with a great love of the outdoor life. Yet even as his food service company expanded, and he initiated plans to diversify into the hotel business, health concerns threatened his success. In 1951, while undergoing an experimental treatment for hepatitis, Marriott developed an acute homesickness for the western ranch of his childhood. He felt that if he were going to survive, he would need the restorative powers of mountains, rivers, and open space.[135]

The Marriotts spent several months riding through the Virginia backcountry looking at land for sale. His desire was a place "to ride a horse in, to hear the morning stillness in." One October afternoon, the couple found Fairfield Farm, just outside the historic village of Hume. The property was located deep in the Virginia hunt country among the rolling foothills of the Blue Ridge Mountains; the Rappahannock River ran along the southern boundary of the farm, and the sloping ridges of Rattlesnake and Oventop mountains framed the northern side. Marriott was immediately captivated by the place:

It looked like a ranch, it looked like the West, at the foothills of the Blue Ridge Mountains about four and a half miles east of the Skyline Drive, east of the Shenandoah range. Beautiful, beautiful country, great grazing country for cattle, sheep, and horses. . . . It had this beautiful old Manor House with brick walls eighteen inches thick and rooms 25 feet square with ceilings 16 feet high.[136]

The brick mansion had been built by James Markham Marshall, brother of Chief Justice John Marshall, on land the brothers had purchased from the heirs of Lord Fairfax. James, a successful lawyer and political figure, received the western portion of the land, instantly making him one of the largest landowners in the state.[137] In 1814 he and his wife, Hester Morris, whose father, Robert, was a signer

OPPOSITE *Oak Spring Garden Library holds Mrs. Mellon's collection of over 13,500 volumes—some dating back to the fifteenth century—on gardening, landscape design, and horticulture.*

ABOVE *A painting by Raoul Dufy hangs alongside Mrs. Mellon's hat.*

A pool house, designed by I.M. Pei, followed, and in 1993, architect Thomas Beach created a sympathetic addition to the library to accommodate Mrs. Mellon's outstanding collection of rare books, manuscripts, art, and artifacts relating to natural history, garden history, landscape design, horticulture, and botany. Although Mrs. Mellon died in 2014 (her husband preceded her by fifteen years) and much of the collection of the house has been dispersed, an endowment also ensures that the Oak Spring Garden Library will remain an invaluable resource for scholars. It also stands as a tribute to Mrs. Mellon's passion for the natural landscape of the Virginia countryside and her belief that "when you go away, you should remember only the peace."[147]

Mount Sharon

Orange County
Charles and Mary Lou Seilheimer

At 930 feet, Mount Sharon is the second-highest point in rural Orange County, exceeded only slightly by Clarke Mountain, which rises to 1,082 feet. Historian W.W. Scott proclaimed, "There are perhaps more picturesque views of the Blue Ridge from other points, but for majestic and rugged outlines there are none to compare with the outlook from Mount Sharon."[157] At its crest Mount Sharon offers a 360-degree view, similar, owner Charlie Seilheimer points out, to the one from Monticello.

Mount Sharon was originally part of land patents granted to brothers John and Francis Taliaferro in 1726 and 1727; the earliest dwelling on the property likely dated to the late eighteenth century. In 1876 Charles Champe Taliaferro inherited the property and in 1890 completed an exuberant Second Empire–style dwelling at the farm. Financial setbacks forced Taliaferro to sell Mount Sharon in 1935 to Ellsworth and Elizabeth Augustus of Cleveland.[158]

By that time the house was in disrepair. Architectural tastes had changed, too, with a renewed interest in Colonial-style buildings fostered in part by the widely publicized re-creation of Colonial Williamsburg.[159] In 1937 the older house at Mount Sharon was replaced by a five-part Georgian Revival house designed by Louis Bancel LaFarge, grandson of noted painter and stained glass artist John LaFarge.[160] The new design combined both traditional forms and materials—brick and Buckingham County slate—with then modern building technology, including the use of reinforced concrete floors, steel framing, and humidification and steam heating systems. LaFarge's attention to craftsmanship is evident in the detailed interior woodwork of his own design, the distinctive mantelpieces over the nine fireplaces, and the architect's precision brass hardware pieces.

LaFarge's plan features a centrally located entrance vestibule that leads into a transverse hall, with the formal dining room to the south and the fully paneled library to the north. The living room, which occupies the full width of the central block, is located on the east side of the hall and features sets of French doors that provide access to the dining and library terraces and the garden beyond.

In the 1950s the Augustuses sold the property, which then passed through several owners until Mary Lou and Charles Seilheimer purchased it in 1995. At the time the Seilheimers lived at Leeton Forest, the 1928 home of architect Waddy B. Wood, in Fauquier County. They enjoyed the rural atmosphere there until, as Charlie says, the city began moving toward them.[161]

When the Seilheimers purchased the eight-hundred-acre Mount Sharon property, the house needed little refinement, so only minor changes were made to "adapt the house for our use," in Charlie's words. The extensive Taliaferro garden,

Mount Pleasant

Surry County
Nicholas and Shelley Schorsch and The Mount Pleasant Foundation

While every farm has volumes of stories to tell, few so fully illustrate the ups and downs of a gentleman's farm over four centuries as Mount Pleasant in Surry County. It is perhaps the best-documented, privately owned plantation in Virginia. Indeed, archaeological evidence of occupation during the Middle Archaic period (6500–3000 BC) suggests that Mount Pleasant's location on the south bank of the James River was a favored place for settlement long before the English arrived at Jamestown, three miles due west, in the seventeenth century.

Among those settlers were Richard and Isabella Pace, who arrived in Virginia armed with a one-hundred-acre direct patent from the Virginia Company of London, along with three hundred additional acres for the use of servants indentured to them. An intact Native Amerian burial plot from the Late Woodland Period (AD 900–1650) suggests that indigenous peoples occupied the Mount Pleasant site not long before the Paces' arrival in 1621. Pace is best remembered for saving the Jamestown colony from a planned massacre in July 1622, when his live-in Native Amerian worker "rose out of his bed and reveales it to Pace, that used him as a Sonne: And thus the rest of the Colony had warning given them, by this meanes was saved."[164] After Richard Pace's death (due to non-massacre causes), Isabella remarried but, widowed a second time, sold the property to neighbor

William Swann in 1635. The Swanns—including magistrate and tavern owner Thomas Swann, dubbed "ye great toad" for his duplicitous role in Bacon's Rebellion[165] —amassed additional land, close to two thousand acres, and documents indicate that several dwellings had been erected on the Mount Pleasant site by the 1650s. Two ill-fated owners later, in 1709, the property was sold to John Hartwell, whose daughter Elizabeth married Richard Cocke IV. Cocke already held substantial property in Henrico and Fluvanna counties, and additional lands in Halifax, Lunenburg, and Blackwater counties followed. One of the criteria by which a farm might be considered elevated to a "gentleman's farm" in the antebellum era is multiplicity; a gentleman had more than one. By this measure, Mount Pleasant certainly attained its gentility under the ownership of Richard Cocke IV. He built the first great house at Mount Pleasant around 1756. Topped with a clipped gable roof, the house was a typical Virginia hall-passage-parlor-type gentry dwelling. One story, with an attic, it wasn't the fanciest house in the colony, but it was notable for its variety of brick patterns, indicating expense and the ambition of permanence; Flemish bond with glazed headers graced the west and south walls, which faced the landside approach, and random glazing featured on the north and east facades, which faced a small garden and the riverfront.[166]

Another criterion for a gentleman's farm is the presence of representational design, of both home

PREVIOUS PAGES *Authentic pickets and rippled glass are evidence of the strict attention to detail in every aspect of the restoration at Mount Pleasant to its appearance during its heyday under John Hartwell Cocke II.*

ABOVE *The 1780 Philadelphia Chippendale desk and bookcase, carved tea table, and later Campeche chair complement the accurately restored woodwork in the formal parlor.*

rescues are turned out every day, with those who need particular care turned out in the "hospital field," where they can be watched from the house. Bogley also has two steeplechase horses, which she trains in The Plains and generally enters in the Iroquois Steeplechase and the Saratoga Springs races. Bogley says she doesn't keep the farm "too manicured," but the farm and its resident animals show that both are well cared for. In 2010 the Land Trust of Virginia awarded Bogley its "Landowner of the Year," recognizing her mindful commitment to maintaining the agricultural nature of her property. When asked why, of all places, she lives out in the remote countryside of Fauquier, Bogley laughs and quotes her former neighbor Paul Mellon, who said, "Nothing beats here!"

ELWAY HALL

Fauquier County
Barry Dixon

Elway Hall's Edwardian elegance, like owner Barry Dixon's design philosophy, is rooted in a deep personal affinity for the landscape and venerable traditions of hunt country living. Built between 1905 and 1907 by Johnson Newlon Camden, a banker, U.S. senator from West Virginia, and "silent" partner in Standard Oil, for his daughter Annie and her husband, General Baldwin Day Spilman of Warrenton, the house retains the evocative outlines and colorful materials of the Gilded Age. At twenty thousand square feet, with ten bedrooms and seventeen fireplaces, Elway Hall was the biggest house Warrenton had ever seen. Annie's brother had commis-

sioned the design when he was elected senator from Kentucky but, finding it too grand, passed it along to his sister.[174] During this period, when other estates in the area were being named, or renamed, to evoke British pastoral imagery—most typically, manors or castles featured in the novels of Sir Walter Scott—Elway Hall is more unusual. The Virginia manor's massive thirty-inch-thick walls—made of native stone from the Lower Harts Mountain quarry—as well as the tower and seemingly artless accumulation of gables, porches, and chimneys convey a more directly material conception of the English gentleman's hunting retreat and its connection to the landscape.

The Spilmans certainly spared no expense in building their own stately Virginia version of an English manor house, drawing on the setting to create a site-specific interpretation of the English Arts and Crafts style of William Morris, Philip Webb, and Charles Voysey. A colorful mix of coursed-stone blocks enlivens the massive masonry walls with pattern, the whole of which is accented with red tile shingles in the gables and a terra-cotta tile roof. The heaviness of the rusticated blocks, recalling the popular American "Richardsonian Romanesque" style of the 1880s and '90s, is further lightened by the verticality of the brick chimneys rising above the roofline, the northeast one featuring an inset stone marker with the date 1907. Just as the architect H.H. Richardson had been inspired by the native materials and geological forms when he developed his eponymous style, Elway Hall's masonry, drawn from local sources, references the property's dry-stacked perimeter stone walls that evolved over two and a half centuries of occupation.[175]

The interior was embellished with a hand-carved oak staircase and not only featured stained glass windows designed by L.C. Tiffany and Company (the company's archives still contain the drawings), but includes a customized portrait medallion of Annie herself, presiding over the stair landing. Nine live-in servants maintained seamless efficiency, lighting fires, cleaning, preparing meals, and responding to the family's calls relayed by means of twenty-two servants' bells. As late as 1930 an article in *Country Life* noted that one full-time staffer's duties were "to wind

OPPOSITE *The elegantly curved staircase extends across the marble-floored entry hall.*

ABOVE *The focal point of the well-appointed Georgian Revival living room is the mantelpiece with its fluted Corinthian pilasters and a "landskip" painting in the framed overmantel.*

Many of the farm's certified or-ganic, certified humane products are sold at Lerner's local pub and at Ayrshire Farm's butcher shop and grocery store.

An avid reader and admirer of Jane Austen, Lerner, under the pseudonym Ava Farmer, is the author of Second Impressions, *the acclaimed sequel to* Pride and Prejudice.

and Gloucester Old Spot pigs, and she owns fourteen Shire horses.

Ayrshire's goal is not to raise the most, but to raise the best. By reclaiming the old breeds and old methods, Lerner says her herds are raised with common sense and less stress. To ensure that her animals are continually well cared for, she has hired a licensed veterinary technician as her livestock manager. Ayrshire is helping to preserve heritage breeds and encouraging better health by better eating.

Lerner is a serious businesswoman and acknowledges that the organic route is more challenging than conventional farming. But in all her pursuits Lerner has approached the conventional in an unconventional way and has enjoyed great success. Ayrshire distributes its products through two outlets owned by Lerner: the Home Farm Store, a butcher shop and deli located in a restored bank building in the heart of Middleburg; and the Hunter's Head Tavern, a pub located in Upperville. Items are also available in many regional restaurants, small organic markets, and online. And although farming in this manner appears more expensive on the surface, Lerner asserts that the real "cost" of conventional farming comes in the pesticides and fertilizers that are applied and that end up in the food supply. Ayrshire relies on the natural fecundity of the Piedmont bluegrass, its own compost for gardens, and less invasive, more sustainable practices to achieve its goals. Ayrshire seeks to raise the best possible food, using methods that can serve as a working model for other farms and that will benefit the safety of the food, the environment, and the family farm. It is sustainability versus profitability.

The farming practices at Ayrshire reflect the classical ideals of the gentleman farmer—by drawing intellectual, physical, and emotional well-being from the surrounding landscape. The pursuit of sustainable farming practices and the humane treatment of animals mean that, at Ayrshire, both the body and the soul are fed.

Salamander Resort and Spa

Loudoun County
Sheila Johnson, Founder and CEO, Salamander Hotels and Resorts

Since 1996 Sheila Johnson—accomplished violinist, photographer, founder of the Black Entertainment Television (BET) network, movie producer (including the award-winning *The Butler*), triple sports franchise owner, and philanthropist—has found that the "natural grace" of the Virginia countryside has held both charm and recuperative powers. Initially drawn to the area by her daughter, an avid equestrian, Johnson has translated the exclusive environment of the hunt country "gentleman's farm" into a distinctive resort destination. Salamander Resort and Spa seems to typify her formula for success: transforming her personal passions into sound businesses.

Johnson's first purchase in the region was Salamander Farm, located in The Plains, which she bought from former Rhode Island governor and telecommunications tycoon Bruce Sundlun—partly to support her daughter's passion for horses and partly as a setting to reinvent herself following a difficult divorce. Sundlun and his former wife, Joy Carter, had named their farm after his World War II code name, which had been granted by his comrades in the French resistance after he survived being shot down and crossing occupied Belgium on foot to reach France. In French heraldry, the salamander not only survives in the midst of fire but emerges renewed. When Johnson bought Sundlun's farm, the name certainly seemed appropriate. "This is perfect," she recalls. And in her characteristic mix of the personal and the entrepreneurial, Johnson adds, "I asked if I could brand it."[188] Sundlun, a savvy businessman himself, recognized a kindred spirit and responded, "Not a problem."

While still busy renovating and expanding this home at Salamander Farm in 2002, Johnson was contacted by a broker who thought she might be interested in another property—a 340-acre estate straddling the town limits of Middleburg, part of the estate of the late ambassador to France Pamela Harriman. Seeing its carefully tended meadows defined by rail and stone fences, its old-growth hardwood trees, and its vistas of the Blue Ridge Mountains to the west, Johnson immediately knew what she wanted to do. Even before the first stone of what became the Inn at Salamander was quarried, she envisioned views of autumn foliage as they would appear from classically inspired windows and imagined flagstone-paved terraces from which to enjoy sunsets in the summer.

Johnson realized that she had the opportunity to share the connection she felt to the architecture, landscape, cuisine, and elegance of the hunt country. She began planning her resort to feel like an extension of her home at Salamander Farm rather than a hotel, placing her own stamp on the age-old tradition of elegant Southern hospitality. She conceived the central block of the resort, with its native

stone masonry and classical portico, as a sibling to that of her own house at nearby Salamander Farm. She recruited Prem Devadas, seasoned hospitality professional and diplomat, to navigate all the complex regulatory processes and to ensure that the resort would meet—if not exceed—even Johnson's high expectations. He understood the importance of detail, down to the use of different coins as spacers between planks to ensure a handmade, vintage quality to the hardwood floors. The personal touch is key: the books in the Salamander Resort and Spa library are from Johnson's own collection; the photographs on the walls are her own work, framed by a local framer; the artwork and music are her choices. These are all reminders that the visitor is a guest, not a customer. The Gold Cup Wine Bar honors Middleburg as the home of the fabled Virginia Gold Cup and International Gold Cup steeplechase races, the running of which have shaped the distinctive hunt country landscape for generations. An emphasis on local varietals and regional vineyards sets the stage for the resort's emphasis on locally sourced ingredients. Even the name of the restaurant, "Harriman's," reflects Johnson's personal take on history. In a fateful encounter in the early 1990s, Ambassador Harriman made a point of waving at Johnson at a crowded event, although the two had never met. Johnson now considers that an omen, a "spiritual blessing" of her eventual stewardship of Harriman's Middleburg estate. Opened in August 2013, Salamander Resort and Spa features 168 guest rooms on four floors, including seventeen suites (named for Johnson's daughter's saddle horses). To heighten the visitor's experience of the landscape, Johnson drew on the colors and textures of the surrounding countryside during the different seasons of the year when conceiving the design for each floor.

In the decade it took to realize her vision for Salamander Resort and Spa, Johnson purchased the Innisbrook Resort near Tampa, Florida, and the Woodlands near Charleston, South Carolina. Two additional Florida holdings have made her hotel company the largest operator of independent golf resorts in the state. With the creation of Salamander, Johnson has moved one step closer not only to her personal vision for the hunt country, but to her entrepreneurial vision to create the "strongest hotel company in the world."[189]

And while many in the elite community feared that Salamander would commercialize the characteristic lifestyle and quiet charm, few can argue with the three hundred new jobs that have been created or the town's new water treatment plant, funded by the resort. In addition, Johnson has placed two hundred of the resort's valuable acres under conservation easement, an investment in the future that acknowledges that the landscape is the essence of the lifestyle Salamander offers to its guests. "This place is really a gift to the town of Middleburg. That is what is so important."[190]

ENDNOTES

PART 1: ESTABLISHING AN AMERICAN TRADITION

1 Charles, Lauren, and Randy Carter, interview by the author, Shirley Plantation, May 12, 2014.

2 Charles H. Carter III, "How Did the Maritime Archaeology Project at Shirley Plantation Begin, and, What Is It Doing?" *Diving into the Past: Shirley Plantation's Maritime Archaeology,* October 2, 2012, accessed at http://shirleyplantationarchaeology.blogspot.com/.

3 Shirley Plantation, *"Be Our Guest!": The Flanker Buildings at Shirley,* September 16, 2011, and October 13, 2011, accessed at http://shirley plantation.wordpress.com/.

4 David F. Allmendinger, *Ruffin: Family and Reform in the Old South* (New York: Oxford University Press, 1989).

5 Robert Carter, letter to his children, as cited in Robert James Teagle, "Land, Labor, and Reform: Hill Carter, Slavery, and Agricultural Improvement at Shirley Plantation, 1816–1866," master's thesis, Virginia Polytechnic Institute, 1998, 9. See also Jennifer Lappas, "A Plantation Family Wardrobe, 1825–1835," master's thesis, Virginia Commonwealth University Theses and Dissertations, 2010, accessed at http://scholarscompass.vcu.edu/etd/2299. The specific chapter "The Carter Family" is available at https://digarchive.library.vcu.edu/bit stream/handle/10156/3156/all%20together.pdf?sequence=1.

6 H. Furlong Baldwin, interview by the author, Eyre Hall, July 28, 2014.

7 Michael Bourne and Marilyn Harper, "Eyre Hall," National Register of Historic Places Nomination Form (2012), section 8, page 16.

8 Bourne and Harper, section 8, page 15.

9 The construction date of the house and other buildings on the farm has been confirmed by dendrochronological investigations conducted by the Oxford Tree-Ring Laboratory (2003) of Baltimore, and also by Mutual Assurance Insurance policies (1756ff).

10 Bourne and Harper, section 8, page 18.

11 Bourne and Harper, section 8, page 21; "model for the man" from Henry St. George Tucker's obituary for John Eyre, as quoted in Fanny Fielding's "Southern Homesteads: Eyre Hall," in *The Land We Love,* vol. 3, no. 6 (October 1867), 511.

12 Although Littleton Eyre's inventory (1768) lists "stamped paper for hanging," it is more likely that John Eyre installed this wallpaper, which the company dates to before 1812. Bourne and Harper, section 7, page 4.

13 J. Thomas Savage, "Eyre Hall on Virginia's Eastern Shore," *The Magazine Antiques* (September 2009), accessed at http://www.the magazineantiques.com/articles/eyre-hall-on-virginias-eastern-shore/.

14 Bourne and Harper, section 7, page 12.

15 Darrin R. Alfred, Garden Club of Virginia Favretti Fellow, Eyre Hall Master Plan (1997), accessed at http://www.gcvfellowship.org /archive.cfm.

16 Victorine Homsey was Mr. Baldwin's cousin. The firm had offices in Wilmington, Delaware, and Boston. Mrs. Baldwin rejected many of the proposed changes that would have compromised the house. Bourne and Harper, section 8, page 24.

17 Dell Upton as quoted in Bourne and Harper, "Eyre Hall," section 8, page 17.

18 George Washington, Diary entry, December 12, 1799, *George Washington Papers 1741–1799,* series 1b, Diaries vol. 36, February 10, 1799–December 13, 1799, Library of Congress; accessed at http://memory.loc.gov/ammem/gwhtml/gwhome.html.

19 Annie Gittess, "Horsemanship," in the *Digital Encyclopedia of George Washington,* ed. Joseph F. Stoltz III, accessed at http://www.mount vernon.org/research-collections/digital-encyclopedia/article/horse manship/.

20 George Washington to James Anderson, December 13, 1799; *George Washington Papers.* Washington notes specifically that after leaving Mount Vernon (Mansion Farm) on the previous day he had visited River, Union, and Dogue Run Farms. Since Muddy Hole Farm lay between River and Dogue Run, the present author has conjectured he would have passed through there as well.

21 George Washington, Diary entry, December 12, 1799, *George Washington Papers.*

22 George Washington to William Strickland, February 20, 1796, as cited in Andrea Wulf, *Founding Gardeners* (New York: Alfred A. Knopf, 2011), 112.

23 Niemcewicz (visit of 1798), as cited by Wulf, 111; Benjamin Henry Latrobe, "A Visit to Washington at Mount Vernon," *The Journals of Benjamin Henry Latrobe* (New York: D. Appleton and Company, 1905), 50–64. Latrobe visited in July 1796.

24 Amada Isaac, *Take Note! George Washington the Reader,* exhibition catalogue (Mount Vernon Ladies' Association, 2013), calculates that thirty-three percent of Washington's book collection of over nine hundred volumes concerned law, economics, and politics, while agriculture and religion tied for second place with fourteen percent each.

25 George Washington to Tobias Lear, May 6, 1794, and other correspondence, chiefly from 1796 and 1799, as cited in Wulf, 111–13.

26 George Washington, "Enclosure: Washington's Plans for His River, Union, and Muddy Hole Farms, 10 December 1799," transcription at *Founders Online,* National Archives, accessed at http://founders. archives.gov/documents/Washington/06-04-02-0403-0002.

27 From the many accounts of Washington's last days, drawn from contemporary sources, the basic chronology and sequence of events here is most indebted to Ron Chernow, *Washington: A Life* (New York: Penguin, 2010), 806–08.

28 Dennis J. Pogue, "The Domestic Architecture of Slavery at George Washington's Mount Vernon," *Winterthur Portfolio 37,* no. 1 (Spring 2002), 5.

29 Wulf, 260, n112 "the Neighbouring Negroes," et seq., notes that Washington voiced this concern in two letters: to David Stuart, February 7, 1796, and to Robert Lewis, August 17, 1799.

30 George Washington to John Sinclair, February 20, 1796, as cited in Wulf, 260, n112 "amusement."

31 George Washington, Diary entry, December 13, 1799, *George Washington Papers.*

32 Washington to Anderson, December 13, 1799, as transcribed in John C. Fitzpatrick, *The Writings of George Washington, from the Original Manuscript Sources,* accessed at http://etext.lib.virginia.edu/washing-ton/.

33 George Washington to Anthony Whiting, January 13, 1793, as cited in Peter Martin, *The Pleasure Gardens of Virginia* (Princeton: Princeton University Press, 1991), 142.

34 Thomas Jefferson, Letter to George Washington, August 14, 1787, extract from the original in the Library of Congress, accessed at http://tjrs.monticello.org/letter/98.

35 Donald Jackson, *Notes from a Year at Monticello, 1795* (Golden, CO: Fulcrum Publishing, 1989), 46.

36 Charles B. Sanford, *The Religious Life of Thomas Jefferson* (Charlottesville: University Press of Virginia, 1984), 41.

37 Sanford, 41.

38 The agricultural writings of Varro, Columella, Cato, and Palladius were often combined into a single thematic volume. Jefferson owned such a volume in Latin published in 1595, bequeathed to him by George Wythe in 1806, as well as another from 1794–97. He also owned a 1771 French translation of the same Latin texts, for which the date of acquisition is unknown. See http://tjlibraries.monticello.org/index.html.

39 Thomas Jefferson, Letter to John Jay, August 23, 1785, extract from original in the Library of Congress, accessed at http://tjrs.monticello.org/letter/69#X3184736.

40 "Origin of the Name Monticello," in the *Thomas Jefferson Encyclopedia*, accessed at http://www.monticello.org/site/research-and-collections/origin-name-monticello.

41 Thomas Jefferson, Letter to William Short, March 29, 1787, as noted in Francis D. Cogliano, *A Companion to Thomas Jefferson* (Blackwell Publishing, 2012); DOI: 10.1111/b.9781444330151.2012.x.

42 While Jefferson's Shadwell library is largely unknown, and he would have had access to a complete classical library at the College of William and Mary, he did own at least one of his copies of Pliny's letters by 1774. The publication data and provenance of these items are noted in E. Millicent Sowerby, comp. *Catalogue of the Library of Thomas Jefferson* (Washington, DC: Library of Congress, 1952–59), vol. 5, p. 7, cats. J16, J17, J18. An English translation owned by Reuben Skelton—*The Letters of Pliny the Younger, with Observations on Each Letter* and *An Essay on Pliny's Life, Addressed to Charles Lord Boyle. By John Earl of Orrery. Volume I. [Volume II. The Third Edition.]* London: printed by James Bettenham, for Paul Vaillant, mdcclii. [1752.]— is documented to have come into Jefferson's library as part of the estate of John Wayles—thus his ownership can be dated to 1773–74. It's not known when he acquired a 1750 Latin edition *C. Plinii Caecilli Secundi Epistolae et Panegyricus Nervae Traiano Dictus*, (Berolini: sumptibus A. Haude et I. C. Speneri, 1750), but a third edition, in Latin, didn't come to Jefferson until 1806, through the estate of George Wythe. According to Sowerby, Jefferson had bid unsuccessfully for this volume at an auction in 1788.

43 Pliny the Younger, letter XXIII to Gallus, *The Harvard Classics* (1909–14), accessed at http://bartleby.com/9/4/1023.html.

44 Thomas Jefferson, letter to Maria Cosway, October 12, 1786, excerpted from a polygraph copy in the Library of Congress, accessed at www.monticello.org/site/Jefferson/workhouse-nature-quotation.

45 Richard, 46, as well as his list of sources, 254–55. See also "Fish" in the *Thomas Jefferson Encyclopedia*, accessed at www.monticello.org.

46 Thomas Jefferson, letter to James Maury, 25 April 1812, extract from original of Jonathan Kasso, accessed at http://tjrs.monticello.org/letter/1835#X3184736.

47 Thomas Jefferson, letter to William Johnson, 10 May 1817, extract from the original at Library of Congress, accessed at http://tjrs.monticello.org/letter/1634.

48 Richard Rush, as quoted in Merrill D. Peterson, *Visitors to Monticello*, paperback ed. (Charlottesville: University of Virginia Press, 1989), 72 ff. and *passim*.

49 James Monroe to William Wirt, April 27, 1826, as cited in Susan Holway Hellman, "Oak Hill: James Monroe's Loudoun Seat," master's thesis, University of Virginia, 1997, 15.

50 Hellman, 17.

51 Hellman, 45, discusses the likely influence and limitations of Monroe's consultations with Jefferson, Latrobe, and even Bulfinch, whom Monroe also knew quite well.

52 Hellman, 39–43.

53 Hellman, 8–14.

54 Edward Ryan, "Oak Hill Buyer, Arlington Native, Began Successful Career in 1929," *Washington Post*, September 3, 1948.

55 Gayle DeLashmutt, interview by the author, at Oak Hill, August 28, 2013.

56 Thomas Jefferson to Gideon Granger, Monticello, September 20, 1810, Library of Congress, *Founders Online*, accessed at http://founders.archives.gov/documents/Jefferson/03-03-02-0061.

57 Hugh Howard has called Poplar Forest's design "a geometry lesson." *Thomas Jefferson, Architect: The Built Legacy of Our Third President* (New York: Rizzoli, 2003), 119. See also C. Allan Brown, "Thomas Jefferson's Poplar Forest: The Mathematics of an Ideal Villa," *The Journal of Garden History,* 10, no. 2 (1990), 117–139; Thomas Jefferson to Elizabeth Trist, April 27, 1806, as quoted in Travis McDonald, "The Private Villa Retreat of Thomas Jefferson," *White House History*, no. 18 (Spring 2006), 19; Travis McDonald, interview by the author, Poplar Forest, July 9, 2014.

58 Howard, 118.

59 John Adams to Thomas Jefferson, letter of introduction for George Ticknor, December 14, 1814, as quoted in Dumas Malone, *The Sage of Monticello* (Boston: Little, Brown and Company, 1981), 164.

60 Travis McDonald, lecture at University of Virginia Club of Richmond luncheon, Bull and Bear Club, Richmond, VA, January 22, 2015. McDonald points out that the seclusion of Poplar Forest, the most private of Jefferson's homes, allowed him to focus on his development of the University of Virginia, which was his most public architectural creation.

61 Other influences on Poplar Forest's design came from architectural books depicting the designs of James Gibbs, William Kent, and Robert Morris. See Howard, 119, 128–29, and McDonald, 7.

62 Timothy Trussell, "A Landscape for Mr. Jefferson's Retreat," in Barbara J. Heath and Jack Gary, eds., *Jefferson's Poplar Forest: Unearthing a Virginia Plantation* (Gainesville: University Press of Florida, 2012), 80–81.

63 Barboursville and Edgemont are among the houses where Jefferson created the appearance of a one-story building by setting the house into the hillside.

64 McDonald, as quoted in Deborah Holmes, "Thomas Jefferson's Poplar Forest," Old House Web, accessed at http://www.oldhouseweb.com/architecture-and-design/thomas-jeffersons-poplar-forest.shtml.

65 James Coles Bruce to James Bruce (1826), as quoted in Clifton Coxe Ellis, "Building Berry Hill: Plantation Houses and Landscapes in Antebellum Virginia," PhD dissertation, University of Virginia, 2000, 45.

66 Halifax County Will Book, 18:183.

67 The sale of Berry Hill resulted from Edward Coles Carrington's debt to James Bruce, which by 1840 had grown to $47,000. James Coles Bruce, acting as executor of his father's estate, persuaded his cousin to sell the property to satisfy the debt. See Ellis, 47; Halifax County Deed Book, 47:138.

68 A copy of the contract is in the Bruce Family Papers held in the Special Collections, University of Virginia. See Ellis, 83–86; Henry W. Lewis, *More Taste Than Prudence: A Study of John Evans Johnson (1815–1870), An Amateur with Patrons* (Chapel Hill, NC: The Borderer Press, 1983), 6–23, 30.

69 Roger Kennedy, *Greek Revival America* (New York: Stewart Tabori & Chang, 1989), 206–07.

70 Lewis Mumford, *Sticks and Stones: A Study of American Architecture*

and Civilization (1924; repr., New York: Dover Publications, Inc., 1955), 22.

71 Ellis, 94–95, 102.

72 Robert E. Lee, *Memoirs of Robert E. Lee, His Military and Personal History,* Marcus J. Wright, ed. (New York: J.M. Stoddart & Co., 1886), 139. Digital edition accessed at www.archive.org. In Lee's letter "the one we so loved" refers to Arlington House, seized by federal troops in May 1861. It was begun by his father-in-law, George Washington Parke Custis in 1802 as a residential tribute to his adoptive grandfather, George Washington. Following his father-in-law's death in 1857, Lee became master of its land, its buildings, and its enslaved people.

73 Charles Royster, *Light Horse Harry Lee and the Legacy of the American Revolution* (Baton Rouge: Louisiana State University Press, 1994), 57. As cited in Myron Magnet, *The Founders at Home: The Building of America, 1735–1817* (New York: W.W. Norton, 2013), 83, n121.

74 Edmund Jennings Lee, *Lee of Virginia, 1642–1892, Biographical and Genealogical Sketches of the Descendants of Colonel Richard Lee* (Philadelphia: Published by Author, 1895; Baltimore: Genealogical Publishing Co., Inc., 1983), 119–20. As cited in Ken McFarland, "Restoration of the Grounds and Gardens at Stratford Hall Plantation," *Magnolia: The Bulletin of the Southern Garden History Society* 19, no. 1 (Winter–Spring 2004), 4.

75 William Henry Fitzhugh, Declaration for Assurance, no. 1608, Mutual Assurance Society, July 25, 1815, and Alexandria Land and Personal Property Tax Records, as cited in Massey Maxwell Associates, "Potts–Fitzhugh House/Robert E. Lee Boyhood Home," National Register of Historic Places Nomination Form, 1985. Wright, in *Memoirs of Robert E. Lee*, 24, notes that the family initially lived on Cameron Street and subsequently another house "known as The Parsonage." Alexandria Land and Personal Property Tax Records document two separate periods of residence for Ann Carter Lee and her children at 607 Oronoco: 1811–16 and again, following the death of Lighthorse Harry Lee, from 1820 to 18 25.

76 Elizabeth Brown Pryor and Robert Edward Lee, *Reading the Man: A Portrait of Robert E. Lee through His Private Letters* (New York: Penguin, 2007), 35.

77 Armes, "Notes on Grounds and Gardens," 1933, no. 7. "1817—Unpublished Verse about Stratford by Charles Carter Lee Written at Harvard University, Cambridge, Massachusetts, in the Year 1817," 4, as cited by McFarland, 4.

78 Stratford Archives, folder containing "Historic References to Stratford's Landscape," quoted material attributed to Charles Carter Lee, Papers, Box 9, second folder after Tibbs vs. Hardy; sheet 12, as cited in McFarland, 4. McFarland also notes that Lee's "aspins" were actually beech trees. The landscape Charles evokes is one of refinement, beauty, and bounty, an enduring impression honed in its presentation by his classical training at Harvard. In 1858, in fact, Charles Carter Lee published *Virginia Georgics*, patently his own native version of the Latin poet Virgil's agricultural poetry cycle, *The Georgics* (c. 29 BC). See Charles Carter Lee, *Virginia Georgics, Written for the Hole and Corner Club of Powhatan* (Richmond: James Woodhouse and Company, 1858).

79 Letter from Eleanor (Nelly) Custis Lewis to Elizabeth Bordley Gibson, March 22, 1821, as cited in Pryor, 36, n91.

80 Umbra, "A Visit to Stratford Hall," *Southern Literary Messenger* (December 1840), vol. VI (Richmond, VA), 801, 803, as cited in McFarland, 5. McFarland also cites an 1871 visit by journalist George Beale

81 Robert E. Lee, *Memoirs*, 139.

82 Robert E. Lee, biography of the author, in *Henry Lee, Memoirs of the War in the Southern Department of the United States* (New York: University Publishing Co., 1869), 41, accessed at www.hathitrust.org.

PART 2: REINVENTING AND REFINING TRADITION

83 Walker partnered with Peter Jefferson, Joshua Fry, and Edmund Pendleton to establish the Loyal Land Company in 1749, becoming one of Thomas Jefferson's legal guardians after Peter Jefferson's death in 1757. Will of Peter Jefferson, as cited in Dumas Malone, *Jefferson the Virginian* (New York: St. Martin's Press, 1948), 154, 438–39.

84 The early history of Castle Hill here is a greatly condensed version of that which appears in Barclay Rives, *William Cabell Rives: A Country to Serve* (New York: Atelerix, 2014), 30–32.

85 A delegate to the oft overlooked 1861 Peace Conference in Washington, Rives vocally opposed secession, already chosen by seven Southern states, and sought to prevent Virginia and other slaveholding states from following suit. Still, when Virginia seceded, he stayed loyal and served in the provisional and second Confederate Congresses.

86 A Lady of Virginia, aka Judith Page Walker Rives, *Tales and Souvenirs of a Residence in Europe* (Philadelphia: Lea and Blanchard, 1842), accessed at www.archive.org.

87 Judith Page Walker Rives, "Avonmore," *Home and the World* (New York: Appleton and Company, 1957), 18–19, accessed at www.archive.org.

88 William Cabell Rives Jr. had married a Bostonian, Grace Winthrop Sears, in 1849 and lived primarily in Newport, Rhode Island. In 1875–76, Peabody and Stearns designed a High Victorian Gothic house (still extant) on a lot given to her by her father, located at the corner of Bath Road (now Memorial Boulevard) and Rhode Island Avenue. See James L. Yarnall, *Newport through Its Architecture* (Lebanon, NH: University Press of New England, 2005), 97.

89 George Lockhart Rives, "Genealogical Notes, Collected by George Lockhart Rives," presented to the New York Public Library, 1924 (New York: Private Printing, 1914), 15, accessed at www.archive.org.

90 Spencer C. Tucker, ed. *American Civil War: The Definitive Encyclopedia and Document Collection* (Santa Barbara, CA: ABC-CLIO, 2013), 1663, accessed at www.googlebooks.com.

91 George Lockhart Rives, 12–13.

92 According to the Master Foxhounds Association, this revival "meant that the Castle Hill hounds were the first recognized pack to be owned and hunted by an American woman." See Norman Fine, "Tally-ho Back! Foxhunting in North America and the MFHA," in *A Centennial View: Foxhunting in America Today* (Lanham, MD: Derrydale Press, 2010), 3. While many sources state that she became the first woman to earn the title Master of Hounds, Mrs. Potts' headstone at Grace Episcopal Church Cemetery in Cismont—a presumably authoritative source—specifies, "Hereditary M.F.H. of Castle Hill Fox Hounds." Allen Potts' book, *Fox Hunting in America* (Washington, DC: The Carnhan Press, 1912), accessed at www.archive.org.

93 Thomas Nelson Page, "To Amelie Rives, on Reading Her 'Grief and Faith,'" as transcribed in Edward L. Tucker, "Thomas Nelson Page's Sonnet to Amelie Rives," *Mississippi Quarterly*, 54, no. 1 (December 2000/2001), 69, accessed at www.proquest.com.

94 Amelie Rives, *The Quick or the Dead? Lippincott's Monthly Magazine* (April 1888), 440, accessed at www.openlibrary.com.

95 Any discussion of Amélie Rives is entirely indebted to Donna M.

Lucey, *Archie and Amélie: Love and Madness in the Gilded Age* (New York: Three Rivers/Crown, 2007). For the romantic cultural construct of reunion, see Nina Silber, *The Romance of Reunion* (Chapel Hill: University of North Carolina Press, 1993).

96 Edward C. Mead, "Merrie Mill," *Historic Homes of the South-west Mountains, Virginia* (Philadelphia: Lippincott, 1899), 175–86, accessed at www.archive.org.

97 Lucey, 276–77.

98 Obituaries, "Class of '96: George Barclay Rives," *Princeton Alumni Weekly*, May 17, 1935, 675.

99 [George] Barclay Rives, letter to Waddy B. Wood, April 9, 1911, Schornberg collection.

100 The Waddy B. Wood papers are housed in the Manuscript Division of the Library of Congress, with finding aid available at http://lccn.loc.gov/mm95082992.

101 William T. Stevens, *Virginia House Tour, Mainly in the Locale Known as Mr. Jefferson's Country* (Charlottesville, VA: W.T. Stevens, 1962), 52.

102 Karen Kennedy, *Morven Park: A Landscape Legacy* (Richmond: The Garden Club of Virginia, 2009), 15–16.

103 Although Swann was himself a successful businessman and lawyer, his endeavors at Morven Park also may have been financed in part by his wife's wealth. When they wed in 1834, Elizabeth Gilmor Sherlock was Baltimore's wealthiest heiress. Aimee Robertson, "The Swann Family: Builders of Morven Park," in *The Bulletin of the Loudoun County Historical Society*, 2004, 11, as quoted in Kennedy, 18. Italianate alterations, designed by the Baltimore architectural firm of Lind & Murdoch, are depicted in a watercolor illustration. Landscape designer Howard Daniels may have advised Swann on the grounds.

104 Davis' paternal family was well established in South Carolina gentry, and his maternal family, the Morrises, was from Gloucester County, Virginia. Both families had expanded their holdings into the Deep South during the 1820s. Davis' place of birth is unclear. One version states that he was born aboard ship while the Davis family was on its annual European vacation. Another states he was born in Paris, and another that he was born in Virginia. Jack Temple Kirby, *Westmoreland Davis: Virginia Planter–Politician, 1859–1942* (Charlottesville: University Press of Virginia, 1968), 8, 20; Carolyn Green, *Morley: The Intimate Story of Virginia's Governor & Mrs. Westmoreland Davis* (Leesburg, VA: Goose Creek Productions, 1998), 7, n13.

105 James Renwick Jr., the architect of the Smithsonian Castle and St. Patrick's Cathedral, along with his partners Aspinwall and Russell, designed Davis' Tuxedo Park home.

106 See Kirby, 25–45; Kennedy, 45.

107 In total, Marguerite estimated that they spent more than eight thousand dollars on boxwoods and yews, but this is likely a low estimate. Green, 84; Kirby, 87–88.

108 Gibson Fisher was hired to build the brick mausoleum in the garden. Westmoreland was placed in the center, his mother, Annie, to one side, and his wife, Marguerite, on the other side. Green, 91–92.

109 Teresa Davenport, "Farming Makes a Welcome Return to Morven Park," July 15, 2013, accessed on Morven Park website, http://www.morvenpark.org/about/news.html/article/2013/06/15/farming-makes-a-welcome-return-to-morven-park.

110 Walter A. Dyer, "Country Life in Loudoun County," *Country Life in America*, February 1908, 385, as quoted in Kennedy, 83.

111 Cheryl Shepherd, "North Wales," National Register of Historic Places Nomination Form, 1999, section 8, page 19.

112 Shepherd, section 8, pages 17–20. See also David D. Plater, "Building the North Wales Mill of William Allason," *The Virginia Magazine of History and Biography* 85, no. 1 (January 1977), 45–50. The Allasons lived in Falmouth in the wintertime.

113 "North Wales Hunt Club Rich in Virginia Tradition," *Washington Post*, January 24, 1935.

114 Christine Sadler, "North Wales Hunt Club Opens Soon," *Washington Post*, October 2, 1938.

115 For examples, see "Miss McConnell's Debut," *Washington Post*, December 30, 1938; "Miss R. Barrett Makes Debut," *Washington Post*, January 1, 1938.

116 Anne Hagner, "Vast Rolling Acres Where Foxes Ran," *Washington Post*, March 26, 1943.

117 Hope Ridings Miller, "Thomas Leiter's Dance Sets Precedent of Fun," *Washington Post*, May 28, 1940.

118 Nina Carter Tabb, "The Hunt Country," *Washington Post*, April 21, 1941.

119 Hagner, "Vast Rolling Acres."

120 "Our History: Walter Chrysler, Jr.," website of the Chrysler Museum, Norfolk, Virginia, accessed at http://www.chrysler.org/about-the-museum/our-history/walter-chrysler-jr/.

121 "Warrenton's Clubs Ready to Exclude Bombs," *Washington Post*, January 24, 1942, 12.

122 Hagner, "Vast Rolling Acres…".

123 Hope Wallach Porter as quoted in Eugene Scheel, "Early Preservationist Recalls Her Finest 'Moment,'" *Washington Post*, October 7, 2007, accessed at www.washingtonpost.com.

124 Johnston was a friend of Grigg's aunt, and she asked him to help her find notable buildings due to his knowledge of historic Virginia houses. Marian Page, *Historic Houses Restored and Preserved* (New York: Whitney Library of Design, 1976), 99. Johnston's photographs comprising the Carnegie Survey of the Architecture of the South, including Edgemont, are at the Library of Congress: http://www.loc.gov/pictures/collection/csas/.

125 Virginia Historic Landmarks Commission (VHLC) Staff, "Edgemont," National Register of Historic Places Nomination, 1980, section 8.

126 Page, *Historic Houses*, 102.

127 James Powell Cocke Southall, "Malvern Hills (*sic*), Henrico County, and Edgemont, Albemarle County, Homes of James Powell Cocke," *Virginia Magazine of History and Biography,* 43 (January 1935), 74–91, 159. Southall was the grandson of James Powell Cocke's youngest daughter.

128 Kimball had ascribed drawings K171-174 to Shadwell, Jefferson's boyhood home that burned in 1770. His reassignment of these drawings to Edgemont was further confirmed by Grigg's discovery of Cocke's Mutual Assurance Insurance policy (No. 349) of 1797, which depicted a sketch floor plan of the dwelling. VHLC, section 8; Fiske Kimball to Milton Grigg, Philadelphia, November 1, 1935, University of Virginia, Special Collections, Papers of Milton L. Grigg.

129 Grigg practiced architecture in Charlottesville from the 1930s through 1964. Joseph LaSala, "Milton LaTour Grigg: The Curriculum Vitae of a Classicist," *Magazine of Albemarle County History* 67 (2009), 14–51.

130 At Edgemont Grigg inserted a staircase salvaged from a house in Charlottesville that was being demolished. Page, 105.

131 Page, 105.

132 Notes on photographs of Edgemont, located in Milton L. Grigg Papers, University of Virginia, Special Collections; LaSala, 27.

133 The de Barroses capture the stories of their circumnavigations in-

Patrick and Arlette Monteiro de Barros' "In the Wake of Charles Darwin: The Seljm's Voyage" (Francoise Heusser Art and Enterprise, 2008).

[134] As quoted in Jennifer Kramer, "Historic Architecture: Edgemont: A Jeffersonian Riddle in Virginia," *Architectural Digest* 53, no. 6 (June 1996), 78. A biography of Dr. de Barros can be found in Lyon Gardiner Tyler, ed., *Encyclopedia of Virginia Biography, Volume II* (New York: Lewis Historical Publishing Company, 1915), 229–30.

[135] Robert O'Brien, *Marriott: The J. Willard Marriott Story* (Salt Lake City, UT: Deseret Book Company 1990), 216–17.

[136] O'Brien, 218.

[137] The Marshall family's ties to Fauquier extend back to 1763, when Thomas Marshall purchased his lease of Fairfax lands and built his home known as The Hollow, located just north of Markham. Many direct descendants of the Marshalls still live in the area in homes established by their ancestors. Fairfax died in 1781 and left a large portion of his American landholdings to his nephew Denny Martin Fairfax. By the end of the nineteenth century, Fairfax agreed to sell the holdings to the Marshall Syndicate; the transactions included well over 160,000 acres. With additional lands that James Marshall purchased from Fairfax, he held over 80,000 acres. See Harry Connelly Groome, *Fauquier during the Proprietorship: A Chronicle of the Colonization and Organization of a Northern Neck County* (1927; repr., Bowie, MD: Heritage Books, 2002), 243, n44.

[138] O'Brien, 218.

[139] Notable guests included avid horsemen President Dwight D. Eisenhower, President Ronald Reagan, King Hussein of Jordan, and American cowboy entertainer Roy Rogers.

[140] Lanier Cate, interview by the author, Marriott Ranch, October 29, 2014.

[141] "Marriott Ranch Video," Marriott Ranch website, accessed at http://marriottranch.com/index.cfm?action=history; O'Brien, 220.

[142] Paul Mellon, with John Baskett, *Reflections in a Silver Spoon* (New York: William Morrow, 1992), 258–59.

[143] Rachel Lambert Mellon as quoted in Sarah Medford, "A World of Her Own," *Sotheby's Magazine*, October 23, 2014, accessed at www.sothebys.com.

[144] Mellon, *Reflections*, 225.

[145] Stacy B. Lloyd III, as quoted in "Arts Patron and Confidante of Jackie Kennedy, Dies at 103," *Washington Post*, March 17, 2014, accessed at www.washingtonpost.com.

[146] Rachel Lambert Mellon, *An Oak Spring Sylva* (Upperville, VA: Oak Spring Garden Foundation, 1989), excerpt accessed at www.oakspring.org.

[147] Rachel Lambert Mellon, as quoted in Sarah Booth Conroy, "The House in the Virginia Hunt Country That Is Home to the Paul Mellons," *New York Times,* June 1, 1969, accessed at www.proquest.com.

PART 3: SUSTAINING THE TRADITION

[148] John R. Hailman, *Thomas Jefferson on Wine* (Jackson: University Press of Mississippi, 2006), 394–95; Richard G. Leahy, *Beyond Jefferson's Vines: The Evolution of Quality Wine in Virginia* (New York: Sterling Epicure, 2012), xiii.

[149] A terroir is a distinct wine-growing region that is defined by the characteristics of its geography, soil, and climate and the sum effects those elements have on the product (be it wine, coffee, or wheat).

[150] Luca Paschina, interview by the author, Barboursville, October 15, 2014. Valmarana's wife, Betty, was friends with the Smithers family, who owned the estate in the 1970s and wanted to sell. Valmarana first offered the farm to an Italian friend who wanted to raise livestock. Valmarana objected and said, "No, you're going to plant grapes for wine." The friend deferred to another buyer, and the rest is history.

[151] Paschina interview.

[152] Frank J. Prial, "Virginia Wine Industry, with Long and Erratic History, Revives Again," *New York Times*, July 21, 1976.

[153] Thomas Jefferson, Barboursville: house (plan and elevation), verso, 1817. N5; K206 [electronic edition]; *Thomas Jefferson Papers: An Electronic Archive* (Boston: Massachusetts Historical Society, 2003), accessed at http://www.thomasjeffersonpapers.org/. As the 1969 National Register of Historic Places Nomination for Barboursville notes, "Had it survived as designed, Barboursville would undoubtedly rank as Jefferson's most important residential work beside Monticello, but even in its present state its significance as a relic of one of America's most distinguished architects is not diminished."

[154] Barbour served in the Virginia House of Delegates (1796–1812), as Governor of Virginia (1812–14), as a U.S. senator (1814–25), as secretary of war (1825–28) under President John Quincy Adams, and as minister plenipotentiary to England (1828–29). Charles D. Lowery, "James Barbour, A Politician and Planter of Ante-Bellum Virginia," PhD thesis, University of Virginia, 1966, 331–85.

[155] R.W. Apple Jr., "Jefferson Gets His Wish: At Last, A Decent Bottle of Virginia Wine," *New York Times*, September 13, 2000; Leahy, vi. In 2013 Gianni Zonin was awarded a Lifetime Achievement Award by *Wine Spectator*. In 2001 Luca Paschina was named Wine Person of the Year and in 2014 was named one of the "20 Most Admired People in the North American Wine Industry." In addition, Paschina was inducted as Commendatore in the Order of Merit of the Italian Republic, which recognizes distinction in occupations that honor the Italian people and their heritage.

[156] Barboursville Vineyards Website, "Heritage," accessed at https://www.bbvwine.com/heritage.

[157] William Wallace Scott, *A History of Orange County, Virginia, from Its Formation in 1734 to the End of Reconstruction in 1870* (Richmond, VA: E. Waddy Co., 1907), 213.

[158] Ann L. Miller, "Mount Sharon," National Register of Historic Places Nomination Form, 2013. The initial patents equaled almost two thousand acres; by the time Charles Champe Taliaferro inherited the property, Mount Sharon encompassed 711 acres. Miller also mentions a letter written by Kathleen Newman Taliaferro, one of the last family members to live at Mount Sharon, which describes the gardens and dates them to c. 1770. For an image of the 1880s Mount Sharon dwelling, see Bryan Clark Green, William S. Rasmussen, and Calder Loth, *Lost Virginia: Vanished Architecture of the Old Dominion* (Charlottesville, VA: Howell Press, Inc., c. 2001), 84.

[159] For more on the rise of Colonial Revival during the early twentieth century, see Richard Guy Wilson, *The Colonial Revival House* (New York: Harry N. Abrams, Inc., [2004]), 89–90, 166–73; and Charles B. Hosmer Jr., "The Colonial Revival in the Public Eye: Williamsburg and Early Garden Restoration," in *The Colonial Revival in America* (New York: W.W. Norton & Company, 1985), 52–70.

[160] LaFarge studied architecture at Harvard and Yale and was apprenticed in the notable firms of Delano & Aldrich and Peabody, Wilson & Brown. He opened his own New York office in 1932. During World War II LaFarge was among the many academic and professional staff called upon to rescue threatened works of art in war-torn Europe—the "Monuments Men"—and was a founding member of the New York City Landmarks Preservation Commission. Miller, "Mount Sharon."

161 Charles Seilheimer Jr. and Mary Lou Seilheimer, interview by the author, Mount Sharon, May 5, 2014.

162 Stick also cites among his influences modernist Dan Kiley, with whom Stick worked, and English gardener and expert horticulturalist Russell Page. See Reuben M. Rainey and Marc Treib, eds., *Dan Kiley Landscapes: The Poetry of Space* (Richmond, CA: William Stout Publishers, [2009]) and Russell Page, *The Education of a Gardener* (New York: Random House, c. 1983).

163 Stick's work at a Connecticut estate won a Palladio Design Award in 2003 and the 2011 Arthur Ross Award for Landscape Architecture from the Institute of Classical Architecture.

164 Edward Waterhouse, August 1622, paraphrasing a report by George Sandys, July 1622, "A Declaration of the State of the Colony and Affaires of Virginia," as transcribed in Myra Jehlen and Michael Warners, eds., *The English Literatures of America: 1500–1800* (New York: Routledge, 1997), 139.

165 Surry County records, as cited in Martha W. McCartney, *Virginia Immigrants and Adventurers, 1607–1635: A Biographical Dictionary* (Baltimore: Genealogical Publishing Co., Inc., 2007), 679.

166 Material information and analysis from Nicholas Luccketti/James River Institute for Archaeology, "Mount Pleasant Architectural and Archaeological Complex," Revised National Register of Historic Places Nomination Form, 2007; also see "History," accessed at www.mount pleasantplantation.com.

167 "John Hartwell Cocke II," accessed at www.mountpleasantplant tion.com.

168 Randall M. Miller, ed., "Introduction," *Dear Master: Letters of a Slave Family* (Athens: University of George Press, 1990), 32–34. The "master" of the title is Cocke, and the letters are those of his former enslaved worker Peyton Skipworth.

169 "Sherwood Plantation," NASA Cultural Resources, accessed at http://crgis.ndc.nasa.gov/historic/Sherwood_Plantation.

170 Advertisement, as quoted in Audrey Windsor Bergner, *Old Plantations and Historic Homes Around Middleburg, Virginia and the Families Who Lived and Loved Within Their Walls* (New York: Cornwall Books, 2001), 79; Fauquier County Deed Book 48:63.

171 William J. Mann Jr., "Free Enterprise Sixty Years Ago: Stories for My Grandchildren," unpublished manuscript, as quoted in Bergner.

172 George H. Dacy, "Grass without Weeds," *The Country Gentleman*, February 27, 1915, 381.

173 Janet Hitchen, "Middleburg Humane Foundation," *The Virginia Maryland Dog,* February 17, 2011.

174 Cheryl Shepherd, "Springs Valley Rural Historic District, Fauquier County, Virginia," National Register of Historic Places Nomination Form, 2009, section 8, page 42. The nomination form identifies Annie Spilman's brother, also Senator Johnson N. Camden, as the author of the design of Elway. Johnson Jr. had attended Episcopal High School in Alexandria, Virginia Military Institute (VMI) in Lexington, and the University of Virginia in Charlottesville, so he may have been familiar with Fauquier and its landscape.

175 Shepherd, section 7, page 11.

176 Shepherd, section 8, pages 70–71; "Flashbacks, 50 Years Ago," *Fairfax Times*, April 22, 2003, accessed at http://ww2.fairfaxtimes.com/cms/archivestory.php?id=164835.

177 Barry Dixon, *Barry Dixon Interiors* (Layton, UT: Gibbs-Smith, 2008), 11; Sarah Devaney-O'Neil, "Dining by Design: Barry Dixon Shares Early Influences," October 2012, accessed at http://storibookdesigns.blogspot.com/2012/10/dining-by-design-barry-dixon-shares.html.

178 Quotes from Barry Dixon, unless otherwise cited, are from an interview by the author, January 26, 2015.

179 CharityworksDC, "Elway Hall, Barry Dixon's Manor," *100 Point Vintage Wine Tasting*, brochure, 2011, accessed at www.charityworksdc.org.

180 "Warrenton's Elway Hall: Restored and Ready for Silver Screen Debut," *Free Lance-Star*, Garden Week Issue, April 12, 2001.

181 Rebecca Christian, "Designer Barry Dixon's Garden and Grounds," *Traditional Home*, October 2011, accessed at http://www.traditionalhome.com/gardens/beautiful-gardens/designer-barry-dixons-garden-and-grounds.

182 Organic certification, obtained through Oregon Tilth, means that the livestock operations and crop production meet stringent requirements that prohibit the use of pesticides and specific medications and chemicals in animals. The Certified Humane recognition comes from Humane Farm Animal Care and addresses standards of environment, shelter, management, health, and nutrition through regular certification. Crystal Ritenour, Ayrshire Farm Large Livestock Division Manager, interview by the author, October 3, 2013.

183 Ayrshire Farm website, accessed at http://www.ayrshirefarm.com/AyrshireFarm/AFHome.html.

184 Fauquier County Deed Book 8 Q:501 (September 26, 1912), James A. Buchanan from Richard B. Lawson.

185 Nicholas Lapham, interview by the author, the Farm at Sunnyside, Little Washington, VA, July 31, 2014.

186 Anthony A. Lapham, Nick's father, who died in 2006, was a trustee of the American Farmland Trust, the National Audubon Society, the Environmental Defense Fund, and other environmental organizations. Joe Holley, "Former CIA General Counsel, Environmentalist Anthony Abbot Lapham, 70," *Washington Post*, November 15, 2006. Nick Lapham worked at the U.S. Department of State, held senior positions at Conservation International, World Wildlife Fund, and the UN Foundation, and worked on the reintroduction of wolves into Yellowstone National Park.

187 Kristie Baynard, EHT Traceries, Inc., "Sunnyside," National Register of Historic Places Nomination Form, 2004, section 9 [*sic*], pages 10–11.

188 Joan Tupponce, "Toast of the Town," *Virginia Living*, August 2013, 37.

189 Margaret Morton, "'We Got It Done': Johnson to Unveil Salamander Resort," *Leesburg Today*, August 23, 2013, accessed at www.leesburgtoday.com.

190 Andrew Sharbel, "The House that Johnson Built," *Loudoun Times-Mirror,* August 30, 2013, accessed at http://www.loudountimes.com/news/article/the_house_that_johnson_built123.

INDEX

Page numbers in italics refer to illustrations.

271

Acknowledgments

At Shirley, we are grateful to Charles, Randy, and Lauren Carter for welcoming us back; thanks to Esther White, Steven Bashore, and Dawn Bonner for her very early morning good cheer at Mount Vernon; Susan Stein and Ann Taylor at Monticello; and H. Furlong Baldwin for a fine Eastern Shore welcome at Eyre Hall. Special thanks to Gayle and Thomas DeLashmutt at Oak Hill for their patience and to architectural historian Susan Hellman for sharing her brilliant research; Nicholas and Shelley Schorsch for opening the doors of Mount Pleasant, and David deMuzio and Steve Pulinka for logistical support, fact checking, and general goodwill; Travis C. McDonald for making Poplar Forest irresistible; Luca Paschina, winemaker and host at Barboursville Vineyards; at Berry Hill, Martha Borg, General Manager Bill Kirkhuff, and Lealand Luck; the late Executive Director Paul Reber, Director of Marketing and Public Relations Jim Schepmoes, Karen Lavar, and Farm Manager Chip Jones at Stratford Hall. We are grateful to Stewart and Ray Humiston for sharing Castle Hill; Al and Cindy Schornberg for the warm welcome at Edgewood/Keswick Vineyards; Assistant Director of Development and Communications Teresa Davenport, Director of Preservation and Education Jana Shafagoj, Director of Civics Programming Abby Pfister, Director of Development Suzanne Musgrave, and Executive Director Frank Milligan at Morven Park; Patrick and Arlette Monteiro de Barros, Debby Cara, and Eddie Davis at Edgemont, and General Manager Lanier Cate at Marriott Ranch at Fairfield. North Wales is entering a new era, and we are grateful to David and Pamela Ford for allowing us to rush right in, and to Johnny Lloyd for showing us so many magnificent buildings and landscapes. For the extraordinary opportunity to visit Oak Spring at the end of an era, we extend our deepest thanks to Stacy Lloyd, Ailene Laws, Alexander Forger, and for their hospitality Oak Springs Garden Librarian Tony Willis, Technician Marci Nadler, and Kimberley Fisher. At Elway Hall eternal thanks to the miraculous Barry Goodinson for the introduction; to Leslie Keating for many phone calls and, of course, to Barry Dixon for his elegance, charm, and time. We are grateful to Mary Lou and Charles Seilheimer at Mount Sharon for their hospitality and to landscape architect Charles J. Stick for a stimulating and informative interview. We extend much gratitude to Rose Marie Bogley at Peace & Plenty at Bollingbrook for her seemingly endless hospitality, and to our friends Leslie Hacker, Leah and Jack Ferguson, William and Katherine Strother, George Thompson, and Mary Bryan DeBerry. We enjoyed every minute of our stay at Ayrshire, thanks to Sandy Lerner; thanks too to Vicki Bendure of Bendure Communications, Livestock Manager Crystal Ritenour, Melissa Chaffins and Sheree McDowell, who made and styled Ayrshire's beautiful food, and, of course, the cats! At Sunnyside Farm are Nick and Gardiner Lapham, who graciously shared their stories, time, and wisdom; and even before the Salamander Resort was open, we felt welcomed by Sheila Johnson and her remarkable team, especially Prem Devadas, president of Salamander Hospitality; Matt Owen, corporate director of public relations; and Vanessa Casas, public relations manager. For his determined pursuit of Arcadia and the germ of this idea, wholehearted thanks to Michael Babin, and for encouragement and introductions from the very beginning, thanks to John F.W. Rogers and Deborah Lehr, Walter Woodson, Laura Simmons, Joshua Lakey, and our intrepid photographer's assistant and all-around-great-guy Forrest MacCormack. Special thanks to Dr. Mitchell Merling, Curator of the Mellon Collection and European Art at the VMFA, for his expertise. Last but not least, thanks to the farmers in our own families and to our spouses for their never failing patience and good ears.